SHAKING YOUR FAMILY TREE
WORKBOOK

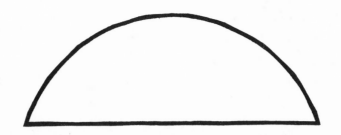

SHAKING YOUR FAMILY TREE

WORKBOOK

a basic guide to tracing your family's genealogy

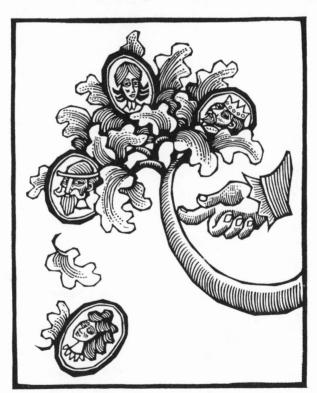

BY MAUREEN ELIZABETH McHUGH
FOREWORD BY DR. RALPH CRANDALL

YANKEE BOOKS

CAMDEN · MAINE

COVER AND TEXT DESIGN BY LURELLE CHEVERIE, ROCKPORT, MAINE
Typeset by Prototype Graphics, Inc., Nashville, Tennessee
Printed and bound by BookCrafters, Chelsea, Michigan

10 9 8 7 6 5 4 3 2 1

Acknowledgments

In the course of putting together these worksheets, I have asked for and thankfully received assistance from a few people whom I'd like to mention here. First, I would like to thank Bob Dunkle, a fellow genealogist, and my buddy, for his input and help; and second, Ann Lainhart, genealogist, for her assistance, and my editors, Sandy Taylor, Mark Corci, and Linda Spencer. I would also like to acknowledge my indebtedness to the late Mrs. Robert Duncan for the wealth of genealogical information with which she provided me. But most of all, my thanks go to my sister, Sharon, who didn't know what she was starting when she introduced me to genealogy, and to whom this book is dedicated.

Contents

Prefatory Note

As more people become interested in "do-it-yourself" genealogy, a greater need arises for functional worksheets. The blank forms contained within this package provide an organized system for you, the researcher, to collect your information. Their purpose is to save you time and money. By using these forms, you will be able to eliminate extraneous material in your genealogical search and limit the amount of time you spend copying various records by hand. You will also save money by avoiding unnecessary photocopying charges.

Please keep in mind that these forms do not teach you how to conduct research, but merely allow you to record genealogical facts.

HAPPY HUNTING!

Foreword

Genealogy, sometimes called "family history," is the third most popular pastime, after stamp and coin collecting, in the United States today. It is estimated that more than thirty million Americans are now engaged in tracing their ancestors.

Why is genealogy so popular? The answer is connected to our being a nation of immigrants. Genealogy satisfies our natural curiosity to know from whom we descend both in America and overseas. Although American families have been tracing their histories since Colonial times, the nation's bicentennial celebrations and Alex Haley's *Roots* stimulated a more widespread interest in genealogy. To-day, people of all nationalities and races are busily searching for their ancestors and discovering that they have contributed in countless ways to American society.

Genealogists are not interested only in discovering "noble" ancestry, or in joining the Mayflower Society or the Daughters of the American Revolution (as worthy as these societies are). Rather, most of us simply want to know who hangs on our family tree, whether he be king, nobleman, or thief. In Australia, where family history is even more popular than in the United States, the goal of most gene-alogists is to prove descent from one of the many convicts sent to that continent from England in the nineteenth century.

Regardless of what motivates you to trace your family, you must develop good research skills to get the most from the experience. Your task is to sift through large quantities of material to find the specific information that accurately identi-fies your ancestors.

What kinds of information should you look for? Basically, whatever will enable you to link one generation to the next, such as a birth, marriage, or death record. Wills often give the names of spouses, children, and grandchildren, thereby link-ing several generations. The challenge is to proceed back in time, generation by generation, until you identify the immigrant ancestors who first planted your family in America. Later you can continue the hunt for ancestors overseas in Old World records.

The search begins at home, interviewing family members and friends and inves-tigating old family letters and documents. Visit or write older family members, friends, and neighbors to glean whatever you can regarding your parents, grandparents, and even great-grandparents. Most family memories extend three or four generations, well into the nineteenth century.

Beyond the interview, you must turn to historical documents for personal data on your ancestors. Remember that historical documents were not designed spe-cifically for the genealogist. Nevertheless, several types of records are genealogically useful. Birth, marriage, and death records—"vital records," as they are called—are especially important. They have been maintained uniformly in all states since at least the turn of the twentieth century. In some areas, such as the New England states, these records are available back to Colonial times. They were originally maintained to preserve inheritances and later to identify illnesses, but they usually contain essential genealogical data. Death records, for example, often give the names of parents, spouses, dates and places of birth, and occupation.

Genealogical records are divided into two basic types—literary and public. Literary documents, such as diaries or letters, are almost always privately owned by individuals, libraries, or historical societies. If available, literary materials can be a gold mine of information. You may own a great-aunt's diary, which faithfully notes weddings, births, and deaths in her generation. Or the local library in your "ancestral seat"—the town where your ancestors first settled or lived for many generations—may have a diary that notes such events for a decade or more for the entire community. Regrettably, such documents are rare. Although you may find one or two literary documents concerning your family, you must turn to public records for much of your information.

Public records are created by public agencies for public purposes. These can be institutional in nature, such as court, church, or educational records; they can be town or selectmen records; or they can be state or national censuses, vital records, or military and land records. They can be created at any level or by any branch of government.

The great value of public records is that they tend to be uniform in nature and cover large sections of the population. The national census, for example, has surveyed all American households at ten-year intervals since 1790. It includes genealogically valuable data such as name, occupation, and (since 1880) birthplace of parents. In some cases, it is possible to use the census to "track" nineteenth-century families that joined the great westward movement and migrated to new homes in the Midwest and West.

Among other public sources, military pensions beginning with the Revolution can provide much genealogical information. Land records at the local and national levels sometimes document several generations of a family, and naturalization papers and ship passenger lists sometimes name the village in the Old World where your immigrant ancestor originated. Certainly one of your major preoccupations as a family researcher will be to learn as much as possible about all types of public records.

Finally, you may be able to use published, or "secondary," sources in your research. An estimated fifty thousand genealogies are now in print, and genealogical information is also found in town and county histories, genealogical and historical society publications, city directories, and newspapers. A portion of this plethora of material is available at your local, regional, state, or university library. The greatest genealogical collections in the United States are at the New England Historic and Genealogical Society in Boston, the New York Public Library, the Library of Congress, the Genealogical Library of the Church of Latter-Day Saints in Salt Lake City, the Newberry Library in Chicago, and the Allen County Public Library in Fort Wayne, Indiana. This genealogical literature will prove essential to your work as a family historian, for part of your ancestry may well have been traced already. You will want to check the published literature for errors, but you can save much time, energy, and expense by using printed sources adroitly.

Very often people involved in genealogy become totally absorbed in it. Their interest becomes keener with the ''hunt,'' and unexpected discoveries concerning many of their ancestors spur them on. I invite you to join this happy group of researchers in learning more about your genealogical past.

DR. RALPH CRANDALL
Director
New England Historic and
Genealogical Society

Tips to Follow in Your Research

Use pencil when you enter data on your genealogical forms. Penciling in your data permits you to amend your records. Also, pencil is made of graphite, making it one of the more durable and permanent markers. Most pens are now water soluble.

Write or print your information clearly. Illegible transcription increases the chance of misreading dates, names, and places.

Note your source. Whether your information comes from Aunt Emma or the National Archives, be sure to cite your sources. Include as much information as possible. Record complete book titles, author's full name, publisher, date of publication, volume numbers, and page numbers. List microfilm publications and roll numbers; write down microfiche publication and card numbers. Keep addresses and telephone numbers of relatives who have supplied genealogical data and family stories. Don't forget to put down the location of your primary source material (land deeds, probates, church records, etc.) just in case you have to examine the original documents again.

If you do not have certain particulars on your ancestor's background, leave the lines blank until you do find that information. Write only the facts you have. Don't speculate on paper.

Examine original documents carefully. Seventeenth-century handwriting styles are different from present styles. Watch your s's and f's. A small s will look like an f in older documents. If you are excerpting an original document, copy it word for word as it is written. Spelling was not uniform until the mid-1800s. Don't assume that your ancestor used one spelling for his name or that the city clerk was infallible. Study all possible spellings for your ancestor's name, the obvious and the not so obvious. Many members within an immediate family circle spelled their name differently even though they were related. Variant spellings and name changes may provide the missing link to your genealogy. Smith might be Smythe, Ranney might be Rainey, and O'Flaherty might be Flaherty. Foreign names were also anglicized. A Norwegian name such as Hejer might be spelled Hayer or Hyer; the French name Langlois might be changed to Langley.

Don't draw conclusions too early. During the course of your genealogical investigations, you will discover contradictory information on some of your ancestors. Usually data that are closer to the time your ancestor lived will prove to be more accurate. For example, a marriage certificate is more apt to be correct than a death certificate. Information on a marriage certificate is provided by the groom and bride, whereas the particulars that appear on a death certificate are supplied by a third party, thereby allowing room for error. This is not to say that all marriage certificates are correct. City and town clerks do make errors, and you should consider this possibility.

To avoid carrying someone else's error, compare and study all your information. Rely heavily on original source records. If you pull information from published family histories, investigate the sources used. A genealogy that does not list its sources of information is not as valuable as one that gleaned its data from town and church records. Don't rely on someone else's analysis unless that researcher has provided the sources that prove his or her case. Rule out the improbable. An ancestor giving birth at the age of 103 is not likely. You either have the wrong person or are missing a few generations. Remember, the more solid evidence you have to support your pedigree, the more it will strengthen your conclusions.

Maintain a duplicate set of source materials and work from these. Keep your originals in a safe-deposit box or a fireproof safe. If one set is accidentally destroyed, you will always have the other as a backup.

Store your original source records (birth, marriage, and death certificates; military papers; census records; land deeds; probate records; family photos and negatives) in proper archival storage materials.

Using the Charts

The Four-Generation Chart

The four-generation chart allows you to establish a flow chart of all your direct ancestors. Direct ancestors are those relatives from whom you are directly descended. For example, son to father to grandfather would be considered a direct relationship. Son to uncle to grandfather would not be a direct line. Direct lines are broken into two categories, paternal and maternal. The paternal line represents the father's direct line, and the maternal represents the mother's direct line.

Look at samples 1 and 2 on pages 17 and 18. All the abbreviations used here are fairly standard among the genealogical community. Here's a brief list for beginners:

Name = name of ancestor
b. = date of birth
bapt. = date of baptism/christening
pb. = place of birth/baptism/christening
m. 1 = date of first marriage
pm. 1 = place of first marriage
div. 1 = date of first divorce (if applicable)
m. 2 = date of second marriage (if applicable)
pm. 2 = place of second marriage (if applicable)
d. = date of death
pd. = place of death
bur. = date of burial
pbur. = place of burial

The spaces to the left of the names are for numbers that serve as easy reference points for you to locate a particular ancestor. Each chart contains space for fifteen names. Number yourself 1; your father 2; your mother 3; your paternal grandfather and grandmother 4 and 5, respectively; your maternal grandfather and grandmother 6 and 7, respectively; and so on. Each father will have a number double that of his child. When you complete the first chart, begin another and label it "Chart 2." Each ancestor keeps his or her number at all times and on all successive charts.

Until you prove your ancestry, you may find or make some mistakes in your initial recordings, and you will want to make corrections. On the back of the four-generation chart (sample 2) is space for you to list the sources of your information. Be sure to write the number of the ancestor for whom you are listing sources. If you received the information from a relative, make sure you include an address in case you want to question him or her further. If you obtained the information from a book, write down the title, author, publisher, place and date of publication, and volume and page numbers. If you abstracted information from an original document, list the type of source (birth record, land record, etc.). Include certificate numbers, docket numbers, and names and locations of these records. Sample 2 is partially filled in to show you how this is done.

Four-Generation Chart

F1

Chart _____

1. Name   **Charles Wells Hale**

   b.   2 October 1838
   bapt.
   pb.   St. Louis, MO
   m. ___   24 August 1859
   pm.   St. Louis, MO
   div. ___
   m. ___
   pm. ___   8 September 1892
   d.
   pd.   Winterset, IA
   bur.
   pbur.

2. Name   **Edward Hale**

   b.   17 February 1802
   bapt.
   pb.   Rutland, VT
   m. ___   11 August 1835
   pm.
   div. ___
   m. ___
   pm. ___
   d.   17 March 1879
   pd.   Hartford, CT
   bur.
   pbur.

3. Name   **Harriet Wells**

   b.   7 August 1812
   bapt.
   pb.   Alstead, NH
   m. ___   11 August 1835
   pm.
   div. ___
   m. ___
   pm. ___
   d.   14 May 1888
   pd.   Orange, NJ
   bur.
   pbur.

4. Name   **Asa Hale**

   b.
   bapt.
   pb.
   m. ___
   pm.
   m. ___
   pm. ___
   d.   2 December 1843
   pd.   Rutland, VT

5. Name

   b.
   bapt.
   pb.
   m. ___
   pm.
   m. ___
   pm. ___
   d.
   pd.

6. Name

   b.
   bapt.
   pb.
   m. ___
   pm.
   m. ___
   pm. ___
   d.
   pd.

7. Name

   b.
   bapt.
   pb.
   m. ___
   pm.
   m. ___
   pm. ___
   d.
   pd.

8. Name _____   see chart _____ #_____

9. Name _____   see chart _____ #_____

10. Name _____   see chart _____ #_____

11. Name _____   see chart _____ #_____

12. Name _____   see chart _____ #_____

13. Name _____   see chart _____ #_____

14. Name _____   see chart _____ #_____

15. Name _____   see chart _____ #_____

LIST SOURCES
ON REVERSE SIDE

SOURCES

1. 16 September 1892 Edit of the Winterset Madisonian - Obit for Charles Hale

2. Madison Co. Dist. Court - death 1910, Book 3, #70, page 50

3. City of St. Louis Marriage Records, St. Louis, MO, Book 9, page 163

4. St. Louis Gen. Soc. Index of St. Louis Marriages, Vol. 1 - 1806-1876

5. Essex Co., NJ Probate Records - Docket #21722 & will adm. for Edward Hale dated 18 September 1891

6. City of Hartford, CT, Vital Records - Death certificate for Edward Hale

7. NJ Vital Records - Death certificate #H82 for Harriet Hale

8. Rutland Dist. Prob. Court - will adm. for Asa Hale

9. Bellefontaine Cemetery Records, St. Louis, MO - int. records - Lot 69 (G-G Grandmother)

10.

11.

12.

13.

14.

15.

The family group sheet is one of the more important and useful genealogical forms. It represents the nuclear family—your ancestor, his or her spouse, their parents, and their children. This sheet will give you an ancestor's individual capsulized history. You can record his or her vital records, military records, religious and political affiliations, the names and vital records of children, plus the names and vital records of the children's spouses. Its purpose is to consolidate various source information in one place and save you from wading through oceans of paper.

A correctly filled-out family group sheet would look something like sample 3 on page 20. Sample 4 shows the reverse side of the family group sheet. Notice that there is a place for you to list your sources. Also on the facing page of the family group sheet, you will find places to enter information regarding additional marriages and divorces (if necessary). Fill in the information on the appropriate lines.

In the lower right corner of the front of the family group sheet, you will see the line "See chart _____ number _____." The numbers to write in these blanks come from your four-generation charts. For example, you might have your paternal great-great-grandfather (ancestor 16) on chart 2, so you would write "See chart 2 number 16."

Family Group Sheet

	HUSBAND	WIFE
Name	Edward Hale, D.D.S.	Harriet Wells
Born	17 February 1802	7 August 1812
Place	Rutland, VT	Alstead, NH
Father	Asa Hale	Shipley Wells
Mother		"Dolly" Randall
Married 1	11 August 1835	11 August 1835
Place		
Divorced		
Place		
Married 2		
Place		
Died	17 March 1879	14 May 1888
Place	Hartford, CT	Orange, NJ
Buried	23 March 1879	18 May 1888
Place	St. Louis, MO	St. Louis, MO
Religion	Presbyterian	Presbyterian
Occupation	Dental Surgeon	Missionary
Military Service		

CHILDREN

# Name	B./Bapt.	Place	Died	Place
1. Edward Jr.	12 July 1830	PA	20 May 1886	Chicago, IL
m. Amelia Chappel	2 December 1830		20 December 1887	St. Louis, MO
child of		at		on
2. Charles Wells	2 October 1838	St. Louis, MO	8 September 1892	Winterset, IA
m. Maria C. Ranney	14 November 1836	St. Louis, MO	28 January 1910	Winterset, IA
child of Nathan Ranney		at St. Louis, MO		on 11 August 1835
3.				
m.				
child of		at		on
4.				
m.				
child of		at		on
5.				
m.				
child of		at		on
6.				
m.				
child of		at		on
7.				
m.				
child of		at		on
8.				
m.				
child of		at		on
9.				
m.				
child of		at		on
10.				
m.				
child of		at		on
11.				
m.				
child of		at		on
12.				
m.				
child of		at		on

See chart _____ number _____

ADDITIONAL MARRIAGES:

Husband m.3 _____ at _____ on _____
     m.4 _____ at _____ on _____
Wife   m.3 _____ at _____ on _____
     m.4 _____ at _____ on _____

ADDITIONAL DIVORCES:

Husband dv.2 on _____ at _____
     dv.3 on _____ at _____
Wife   dv.2 on _____ at _____
     dv.3 on _____ at _____

ADDITIONAL SPOUSE INFORMATION

    husband 2 b. _____ at _____
    child of _____
    husband 3 b. _____ at _____
    child of _____
    husband 4 b. _____
    child of _____

    wife 2 b. _____ at _____
    child of _____
    wife 3 b. _____ at _____
    child of _____
    wife 4 b. _____ at _____
    child of _____

RESIDENCES:

_____
_____
_____
_____
_____
_____
_____
_____
_____
_____

SOURCES:

Iowa Vital Records death certificate for Maria Carr Hale ; 16 September 1892 edition of THE WINTERSET MADISONIAN - obituary for Charles Hale; the Madison C. District Court, Winterset, IA - death 1910, Book 3, #70, page 50; City of St. Louis Marriage Records, St. Louis, MO, Book 9, page 163; St. Louis Genealogical Society Index of St. Louis Marriages, Vol. 1, 1806-1876; Essex Co., NJ Probate Courts - Docket #21722 & will adm. for Edward Hale dated 18 September 1891; City of Hartford, CT Vital Records, death certificate for Edward Hale; New Jersey Vital Records - death certificate #H82 for Harriet Hale; the 22 & 23 March 1879 editions of THE ST. LOUIS POST DISPATCH, Scharf's HISTORY OF ST. LOUIS, MO., Vol. 2, page 1567; the 16 May 1888 edition of the ST. LOUIS GLOBE; Bellefontaine Cemetery Records, St. Louis, MO - interment records for Lot 69; 1840 & 1840 Missouri Federal Censuses; Rutland District Probate Court, Rutland, VT - will adm. for Asa Hale.

Vital records refer to the particulars concerning a person's birth, marriage, and death. All states have departments that house these records. Chapter 3 in *Shaking Your Family Tree* discusses availability of these records.

Vital records provide many clues to earlier generations. Birth certificates often include information on a child's parents, including occupations, ages, and birthplaces. If a birth occurred at home, the address is sometimes listed. Marriage certificates provide clues to the ages and birthplaces of the bride and groom and sometimes their parents and religious affiliations. Death certificates contain information such as date of birth or age of the deceased, spouse's name, information on the deceased's parents, residence at the time of death, occupation and sometimes place of work, and number of years living in the United States if the deceased was of foreign birth.

Exactly how much of this information appears in the records will vary from state to state. If you have the good fortune to be close enough to visit a repository for vital statistics, you will want to take some vital record forms with you to save money. Copies of original vital statistics will cost you one dollar and up for each uncertified photostat or two dollars and up for certified copies. There is no charge to look at the records in person.

Sample 5, 5A, 5B on pages 23, 24, 25 are examples of a birth, marriage, and death record form. Note the space at the bottom of the page for listing sources, if you did not take the information directly from a vital record.

Name	Harriet Wells
Born	7 August 1811
Place	Alstead, NH
If Birth Not at Hospital, State Address	
Birth Certificate No.	352
Father	Shipley Wells
Father's Age	
Father's Birthplace	
Father's Occupation	
Mother	Dolly Wells
Mother's Age	
Mother's Birthplace	
Mother's Occupation	

If not taken from vital records, fill in below.

Microfilm No. _____ Roll No. _____
Microfiche No. _____ Card No. _____

Book Title _____
Author _____
Publisher _____
Publication Date _____
Volume & Page No. _____

Groom	Charles W. Hale
Groom's Age	
Groom's Birthplace	
Groom's Father	
Groom's Mother	
Date of Marriage	24 March 1859
Place	St. Louis, MO
Marriage Certificate No.	9:163
Bride	Maria C. Ranney
Bride's Age	
Bride's Birthplace	
Bride's Father	
Bride's Mother	

If not taken from vital records, fill in below.

Microfilm No. _____ Roll No. _____
Microfiche No. _____ Card No. _____

Book Title ___Marriage Record (License) Book - State of Missouri_____
Author ___Recorder of Deeds - C. Kumle_____
Publisher _____
Publication Date _____
Volume & Page No. ___9:163_____

Name of Deceased	Harriet Hale
Died	14 May 1888
Place	Orange, Essex Co., NJ
If Death Not at Hospital, State Address	123 Cleveland Street
Cause of Death	Malignant ulceration
Burial Date	
Place	St. Louis, MO
Death Certificate No.	H82
Age/Birthdate	75 yrs. 9 mos. 7 days
Birthplace	Alstead, NH
Father's Name	Shipley Wells
Father's Birthplace	
Mother's Name	Dorothea Randall
Mother's Birthplace	Alstead, NH
Marital Status	Widow
Spouse's Name	
Deceased's Residence at Time of Death	Orange, Essex Co.
Occupation	
Years Lived in U.S.	
Citizenship	
Informant	
Relationship to Deceased	

If not taken from vital records, fill in below.

Microfilm No. _____ Roll No. _____

Microfiche No. _____ Card No. _____

Book Title _____

Author _____

Publisher _____

Publication Date _____

Volume & Page No. _____

Another great source of genealogical information is the land deed. Located mainly in county courthouses, land records offer a wealth of information regarding the buying and selling of property by an ancestor. Land deeds contain clues that often lead to an elusive ancestor. Among the data that can be found in land deeds are the former residences of an ancestor, location of current residence, names of children and sometimes their spouses and residences, the name of the ancestor's spouse, and the ancestor's occupation. All this information can supply missing pieces to a genealogy.

Since land records are original documents, the older records are, of course, fragile. In some courthouses, you will be unable to photocopy the original and will have to abstract information. The land record abstract form simplifies this task. For instance, William Shackford of Portsmouth, mentioned in the Rockingham County Courthouse land and probate records, divided some property among his relatives in 1739. An abstract of this information would look like Sample 6 on page 27.

The information for the sample was abstracted from the original courthouse record contained in book 24, page 34. If, however, the date was extracted from a printed book of land abstracts, you should write down the book title, author/editor, publisher, and other bibliographic information next to the word "Source."

State **NH**   County **Rockingham**   Town/City **Portsmouth**

Book Vol. & Page No.	24:34
Grantor	William Shackford
Town of Residence	Portsmouth
Grantee(s)	Paul Shackford of Newbury, Essex Co., MA
	John Shackford of Portsmouth, NH
	of
	of
	of
	of
	of
Description of Property	". . . a certain farme (illegible) of sundry tracts & piecs of land scituate
in Newington in sd. Prov. of N. Hamps: Inclosed in several separate Inclosures lying at some smale Distance one from ye
other where of ye Fathers of ye sd parties Dyed Seizd. - In Comon for divdd. - NOW to ye End a Perpetual Partition of
Division shal be had & made Between ye sd Parties . . ."

Date Filed	22 March 1738/1739
Court Filed	24 March 1739
Recorded	31 March 1939
Witnesses	John Sherburn
	John Wentworth

Also located in county courthouses are probate records. Here you will find wills and will administrations. They are usually indexed by surname. You may have to sign for the probate documents you wish to examine.

As with land records, the older wills are very fragile. Photocopying permission and charges vary from courthouse to courthouse. In most instances, you will want to use a will abstract form. This form enables you to extract pertinent information from probate records for your genealogy. The contents of probate records will vary from case to case, but you should be able to discover some, if not all, of the following: children born to your ancestor; name of a spouse who outlived the deceased; other heirs, which might include brothers, sisters, grandchildren, and others.

A probate might also reveal that the deceased died intestate (that is, without making a will) or insolvent. In such cases, there are will administrations. A court- or family-appointed representative assesses the worth of the estate and includes an inventory, a list of claimants for unpaid debts, and most names (and sometimes locations) of heirs. If minor children are involved, there are documents regarding the names of the children and the appointment of wards.

Let's look at an example. On December 26, 1843, the heirs of Asa Hale, deceased, filed a petition in Rutland District Court that Asa Hale died intestate. Moses Perkins was appointed administrator for the estate on the same day. A call for inventory, a warrant of appraisal, and a commission of claims were issued. An appraiser's report was filed and petitions of licenses issued to pay off debts. A sale of report followed, with the final administration taking place on January 5, 1848. Much of the information contained in the probate records for Asa Hale turned out to be extraneous and was weeded out. The legal papers were condensed into the neat and easy-to-read summary shown in sample 7 on page 29.

Three things should be mentioned here. First, when you are working with a will rather than an administration, include the names of the witnesses on the proper line. Second, if the witnesses or executor/executrix are related to the deceased, note the relationship. An executor to the deceased's will might be his or her brother, or a witness might turn out to be a cousin. Finally, some courts use docket numbers as opposed to a book and page system. Others use both. Make sure you record these numbers in the proper places to avoid confusion.

Name of Deceased	Asa Hale
Vol. No. & Page No.	20:103,136,628; 21:507; 22:197,178
Docket No.	
Date Written	
Date Probated	26 December 1843 - 5 January 1848
Court Where Probated	Rutland District Court, Rutland, VT
Name of Widow/Widower	
Children Mentioned	Asa Hale
	Hiram Hale
	David Hale
	Edward Hale
	Mary Hatch
	Sarah Hale
	Alvinia (Elmira ?) Hale - illegible
	Fanny Dale
Other Heirs & Their Relationship to Deceased	
Executor(s)/Executrix	
Administrator	Moses Perkins
Witnesses	
Miscellaneous Data	Deceased died intestate on 2 December 1843. Moses Perkins
	declared the estate as insolvent 29 December 1843. Only
	heirs living in the state, David & Elmira Hale

If not from original document, fill in below.

Source (if not from a book) _____

_____

Book Title _____

Author _____

Publisher _____

Publication Date _____

Volume & Page No. _____

Sometime in the course of your research, you might not be able to find a death certificate for an ancestor. When this happens, try to obtain burial or interment records from the cemetery or one of the many church record offices. Information contained on the form will give you the lot, section, and plot numbers of your ancestor's grave, along with the date and place of burial. With this information you will be able to find the location of a particular grave in the cemetery and glean information from the gravestone itself. Or you might discover a quaint inscription on the stone that you wish to remember. In any case, jot down all the information on the gravestone. If part of the stone is illegible, put a question mark after the word or date in question so you know there is room for error.

Also consult local libraries in the towns where your ancestors died. Many towns and cities have local cemetery associations that are in the process of cataloguing the gravestone inscriptions of their cemeteries. You might be able to find your ancestor in these local and personal publications and save yourself unnecessary searching in cemeteries.

The burial form in sample 8 on page 31 covers both ancient and modern burials. Whereas lot and section numbers have become common today, some of this information was not used or was lost during Colonial times. Therefore, we have included a section for you to write information from the gravestone itself.

Based on information extracted from the Bellefontaine cemetery records for Edward Hale located in St. Louis, Missouri, we discovered the dates of birth and death plus the cities where these events occurred. We also learned the location of the grave. From these facts, we could visit the grave to check the tombstone for further information such as a spouse's grave, and we could pursue our search based on the new clues provided in the cemetery records. For example, since the cemetery record lists Edward's place of death as Hartford, Connecticut, we could check the vital records of Hartford to confirm this fact.

Name of Deceased	Edward Hale
Date of Death	17 March 1879
Place of Death	Hartford, CT
Date of Burial	23 March 1879
Place of Burial	Bellefontaine Cemetery, St. Louis, MO
Lot No.	69
Section No.	97
Plot No.	14
Owner of Plot	
Owner's Residence	
Deceased's Date of Birth	17 February 1802
Deceased's Place of Birth	Rutland, VT
Tombstone Inscription	

If not taken from original document, fill in below.

Source (if not book) _____
Book Title _____
Author _____
Publisher _____
Publication Date _____
Volume & Page No. _____

Military service records—and especially pension files—also provide a great deal of genealogical information. A pension record contains personal information about the soldier's vital statistics and residence. If the widow filed the pension claim rather than the veteran, she had to prove her marriage to the soldier. Sometimes a soldier's children and/or other claimants appear in the pension files as well.

Don't overlook enlistment and discharge papers for your veteran ancestor. They, too, provide useful genealogical information. A case in point is the original discharge paper of Charles Gordon, a veteran of the Civil War who served as a private with Company E in the 11th Regiment of the New Hampshire Infantry Volunteers. On June 5, 1865, he was discharged from the Union army. His residence at the time of this discharge was the Slough U.S. General Hospital in Virginia. More important, the original document lists Gordon's age as fifty-seven; his birthplace as Epsom, New Hampshire; his occupation prior to service as shoemaker. Sample 9 on page 33 shows a military service record form with this information.

Name of Veteran	Charles Gordon
Serial No.	
State from which Served	New Hampshire
Age/Date of Birth	57
Place of Birth	Epsom, NH
Dates of Service	15 August 1862 - 5 June 1865
Branch of Service	Army **X** Navy Air Force Marines Coast Guard Other
If Other, Specify	
Kind of Service	Regulars Reserves Natl. Guard Volunteers **X** Conscript
If Served in Civil War	Union **X** Confederate
If Served in Revolution	Patriot Loyalist Privateer Foreign Army
If Foreign Army	German French
If Army or Marines Regiment/Brigade/Division	11th Regiment of NH Vol. Inf.
Company/Batallion	E
If Navy or Coast Guard Ship or Shore	
If Ship, Specify Ship(s)	
If Air Force Wing/Squadron	
Commander's Name	
Captain's Name(s)	A.C. Locke
Lieutenant's Name(s)	
Bounty Land File No. (Service prior to 1856)	
Pension File No.	
Military Record No.	
Date of Death	
Place of Death	
Cause of Death	
Widow's Name	
Widow's Place of Birth	
Date and Place of Marriage	
Children	
Other Claimants to Pension & Relationship to Deceased	
Residence after Service Street/City/State	
If Veterans Hospital/Home, Name/Street/City/State	Slough U.S. General Hospital

Source _____ Original discharge paper _____

Microfilm No. _____ Roll No. _____

Microfiche No. _____ Card No. _____

If not from original document, fill in below.

Source (if not book) _____

Book Title _____

Author _____

Publisher _____

Publication Date _____

Volume & Page No. _____

At some point, through your diligent research, you will discover your immigrant ancestor. He or she may have been an indentured servant, a convict, an adventurer seeking new challenges, a pilgrim seeking religious freedom, a political agitator requesting asylum, or an Irish famine immigrant looking for work and food. Until the latter part of the nineteenth century, most of these immigrants arrived on wooden ships, freighters, and carrier lines. These ships kept passenger lists, some more detailed than others. They often include the immigrant's age, occupation, last residence outside the United States, and destination. Sometimes family members traveling together were listed together. All this information will help you identify your immigrant ancestor and perhaps give you a starting point overseas if you wish to continue your research abroad. Sample 10 on page 35 shows a passenger arrival form.

Name of Passenger	Janet McIlroy
Date of Birth/Age	37
Place of Birth	Scotland
Name of Ship or other mode of transport	S.S. Isebella St.
Date of Departure	
Port of Origin	
Date of Arrival	12 July 1849
Port of Entry	Boston, MA
Last Residence	Greenock
Citizenship	
Occupation	wife
Destination	

FAMILY MEMBERS

Sex	Name	Age	Place of Birth
F	Cath	8	
F	Margt	5	
F	Mary	3	

Source _____ National Archives of the U.S. _____
Microfilm No. __265__ Roll No. __173__
Microfiche No. _____ Card No. _____

If not taken from original document, fill in below.

Source (if not book) _____
Book Title _____
Author _____
Publisher _____
Publication Date _____
Volume & Page No. _____

Many of your immigrant ancestors who came to build new lives in the United States became citizens, and, as new citizens, they were required to fill out a naturalization record, usually in the court nearest to their residence. If naturalization occurred after 1906, you should write the Immigration and Naturalization Service. Earlier records are divided among federal, state, and local courts.

The most important piece of information the naturalization record will tell you is the town and/or county from which your ancestor came. For many amateur family genealogists, this is one of the greatest stumbling blocks. Too often, ship passenger lists mention only the country from which an immigrant came. Naturalization records sometimes solve this problem.

How do you know whether or not your ancestor was naturalized? If he or she was an immigrant between the years 1850 and 1900, check the census records, especially the 1900 federal census if your ancestor traveled to the United States after 1880. Once you have established that your immigrant ancestor became a citizen, you may begin your search for naturalization papers. Sample 11 on page 37 shows a naturalization record form.

Name	
Date of Birth	
Place of Birth	
Last Address Outside U.S.	
Alien Registration No.	
Name of Ship	
Port of Departure	
Date of Departure	
Port of Entry	
Other Mode of Travel Used to Enter U.S.	
Date of Arrival	
Name Used at Time of Entry	
Name Used on Naturalization Cert.	
Naturalization Certificate No.	
Name of Naturalization Court	
Location of Court	
Residence at Time of Naturalization	
Street	
City & State	

Source _____

Microfilm No. _____ Roll No. _____

Microfiche No. _____ Card No. _____

If not taken from original document, fill in below.

Source (if not book) _____

Book Title _____

Author _____

Publisher _____

Publication Date _____

Volume & Page No. _____

The federal census, begun in 1790, is conducted every ten years. Because census records are restricted for seventy-two years to protect the privacy of living persons, only censuses to the year 1910 are available for research at this time. These records hold vast amounts of information. From census records you are able to learn information such as the names of children, a wife's name, occupation, immigration years (in 1900 and 1910 censuses), citizenship, birthplace, and parents' birthplaces. Remember that not every census contains the same information, but all will be helpful to you. Key censuses are those from 1850 to 1910 because they contain the most data concerning your relatives. Older records are also valuable because they pinpoint where your relatives were and allow you to continue your research in town, church, and county records.

The 1890 federal census was lost in a fire, making the 1880 and 1900 censuses critical sources of information. Sample 12 on page 39 uses information from a microfilm of the original 1880 Rhode Island federal census. This particular census includes the names of all residents at a given address, their race, sex, age, relationship to the head of household, marital status, occupation, literacy, birthplace, and parents' birthplaces.

At the top of the form you will find a place to note your source. In this case, the source is microfilm. On the microfilm will be one or two numbers. The first number is generally the source number and the second the roll number. The sample has only a source number, T9–1216. If your source is a book, write down the title, editor/compiler, publisher, publication date, volume (if necessary), and page number.

To locate your ancestor, you should try to have two pieces of information—the town or city and the state where your ancestor lived. If you do not know the town or city, try to establish the county of residence. This will make your search of census records much easier, as individuals are listed by residence, not according to the last name.

1880 Federal Census

State __Rhode Island__ County __Providence__ City/Town __Woonsocket__

District/Ward/Beat ____

Sup. Dist. No. __121__ Enumeration Dist. No. __142__ Post Office ____ Page __27__ Line(s) __17-19__

Book Title ____ Enumeration Date __6/8/1880__ Microfilm/Microfiche No. __T9-1216__ Roll/Card No. ____

Publisher ____ Author/Editor ____ Volume No. ____ Page No. ____

Publication Date ____

House No. & Street	Family No.	Names of Residents	Color	Sex	Age prior to June 1	Month of birth if born census year	Relationship to head of household	Single	Married	Widowed	Divorced	Married in census year	Occupation	Cannot read	Cannot write	Birthplace	Father's birthplace	Mother's birthplace
	221	Briggs, James	W	M	35				X				works in cotton mills			RI		
		Elizabeth	W	F	28		wife		X				keeping house			RI	ENG	ENG
		Ida	W	F	10		daughter	X					at school			RI	RI	RI

Charts for
Your Use

Four-Generation Chart

Chart _____

8. Name _____
see chart _____ #

9. Name _____
see chart _____ #

10. Name _____
see chart _____ #

11. Name _____
see chart _____ #

12. Name _____
see chart _____ #

13. Name _____
see chart _____ #

14. Name _____
see chart _____ #

15. Name _____
see chart _____ #

4. Name _____
b. _____
bapt. _____
pb. _____
m. _____
pm. _____
m. _____
pm. _____
d. _____
pd. _____

5. Name _____
b. _____
bapt. _____
pb. _____
m. _____
pm. _____
m. _____
pm. _____
d. _____
pd. _____

6. Name _____
b. _____
bapt. _____
pb. _____
m. _____
pm. _____
m. _____
pm. _____
d. _____
pd. _____

7. Name _____
b. _____
bapt. _____
pb. _____
m. _____
pm. _____
m. _____
pm. _____
d. _____
pd. _____

2. Name _____
b. _____
bapt. _____
pb. _____
m. _____
pm. _____
div. _____
m. _____
pm. _____
d. _____
pd. _____
bur. _____
pbur. _____

3. Name _____
b. _____
bapt. _____
pb. _____
m. _____
pm. _____
div. _____
m. _____
pm. _____
d. _____
pd. _____
bur. _____
pbur. _____

1. Name _____
b. _____
bapt. _____
pb. _____
m. _____
pm. _____
div. _____
m. _____
pm. _____
d. _____
pd. _____
bur. _____
pbur. _____

LIST SOURCES
ON REVERSE SIDE

SOURCES

1. _____

_____

_____

2. _____

_____

_____

3. _____

_____

_____

4. _____

_____

_____

5. _____

_____

_____

6. _____

_____

_____

7. _____

_____

_____

8. _____

9. _____

10. _____

11. _____

12. _____

13. _____

14. _____

15. _____

Family Group Chart

	HUSBAND	WIFE
Name		
Born		
Place		
Father		
Mother		
Married 1		
Place		
Divorced		
Place		
Married 2		
Place		
Died		
Place		
Buried		
Place		
Religion		
Occupation		
Military Service		
CHILDREN		

# Name	B./Bapt.	Place	Died	Place
1.				
m.				
child of		at		on
2.				
m.				
child of		at		
3.				
m.				
child of		at		on
4.				
m.				
child of		at		on
5.				
m.				
child of		at		on
6.				
m.				
child of		at		on
7.				
m.				
child of		at		on
8.				
m.				
child of		at		on
9.				
m.				
child of		at		on
10.				
m.				
child of		at		on
11.				
m.				
child of		at		on
12.				
m.				
child of		at		on

See chart _____ number _____

ADDITIONAL MARRIAGES:

Husband m.3 _____ at _____ on _____
       m.4 _____ at _____ on _____
Wife   m.3 _____ at _____ on _____
       m.4 _____ at _____ on _____

ADDITIONAL DIVORCES:

Husband dv.2 on _____ at _____
       dv.3 on _____ at _____
Wife   dv.2 on _____ at _____
       dv.3 on _____ at _____

ADDITIONAL SPOUSE INFORMATION

    husband 2 b. _____ at _____
    child of _____
    husband 3 b. _____ at _____
    child of _____
    husband 4 b. _____ at _____
    child of _____

    wife 2 b. _____ at _____
    child of _____
    wife 3 b. _____ at _____
    child of _____
    wife 4 b. _____ at _____
    child of _____

RESIDENCES:

_____
_____
_____
_____
_____
_____
_____
_____
_____

SOURCES:

_____
_____
_____
_____
_____
_____
_____
_____
_____
_____

Birth Record Form

Name	
Born	
Place	
If Birth Not at Hospital, State Address	
Birth Certificate No.	
Father	
Father's Age	
Father's Birthplace	
Father's Occupation	
Mother	
Mother's Age	
Mother's Birthplace	
Mother's Occupation	

If not taken from vital records, fill in below.

Microfilm No. _____ Roll No. _____
Microfiche No. _____ Card No. _____

Book Title _____
Author _____
Publisher _____
Publication Date _____
Volume & Page No. _____

Groom	
Groom's Age	
Groom's Birthplace	
Groom's Father	
Groom's Mother	
Date of Marriage	
Place	
Marriage Certificate No.	
Bride	
Bride's Age	
Bride's Birthplace	
Bride's Father	
Bride's Mother	

If not taken from vital records, fill in below.

Microfilm No. _____ Roll No. _____
Microfiche No. _____ Card No. _____

Book Title _____
Author _____
Publisher _____
Publication Date _____
Volume & Page No. _____

Death Record Form

Name of Deceased	
Died	
Place	
If Death Not at Hospital, State Address	
Cause of Death	
Burial Date	
Place	
Death Certificate No.	
Age/Birthdate	
Birthplace	
Father's Name	
Father's Birthplace	
Mother's Name	
Mother's Birthplace	
Marital Status	
Spouse's Name	
Deceased's Residence at Time of Death	
Occupation	
Years Lived in U.S.	
Citizenship	
Informant	
Relationship to Deceased	

If not taken from vital records, fill in below.

Microfilm No. _____ Roll No. _____
Microfiche No. _____ Card No. _____

Book Title _____
Author _____
Publisher _____
Publication Date _____
Volume & Page No. _____

Land Record Abstract Form

State _____ County _____ Town/City _____

Book Vol. & Page No.	
Grantor	
Town of Residence	
Grantee(s)	of
	of
	of
	of
	of
	of
	of
Description of Property	
Date Filed	
Court Filed	
Recorded	
Witnesses	

Name of Deceased	
Vol. No. & Page No.	
Docket No.	
Date Written	
Date Probated	
Court Where Probated	
Name of Widow/Widower	
Children Mentioned	
Other Heirs & Their Relationship to Deceased	
Executor(s)/Executrix	
Administrator	
Witnesses	
Miscellaneous Data	

If not from original document, fill in below.

Source (if not from a book) _____

_____

Book Title _____

Author _____

Publisher _____

Publication Date _____

Volume & Page No. _____

Name of Deceased	
Date of Death	
Place of Death	
Date of Burial	
Place of Burial	
Lot No.	
Section No.	
Plot No.	
Owner of Plot	
Owner's Residence	
Deceased's Date of Birth	
Deceased's Place of Birth	
Tombstone Inscription	

If not taken from original document, fill in below.

Source (if not book) _____

Book Title _____

Author _____

Publisher _____

Publication Date _____

Volume & Page No. _____

Military Service Record

Name of Veteran	
Serial No.	
State from which Served	
Age/Date of Birth	
Place of Birth	
Dates of Service	

Branch of Service	Army Navy Air Force Marines Coast Guard Other
If Other, Specify	

Kind of Service	Regulars Reserves Natl. Guard Volunteers Conscript
If Served in Civil War	Union Confederate

If Served in Revolution	Patriot Loyalist Privateer Foreign Army
If Foreign Army	German French

If Army or Marines Regiment/Brigade/Division	
Company/Batallion	
If Navy or Coast Guard Ship or Shore	
If Ship, Specify Ship(s)	
If Air Force Wing/Squadron	
Commander's Name	
Captain's Name(s)	
Lieutenant's Name(s)	
Bounty Land File No. (Service prior to 1856)	
Pension File No.	
Military Record No.	
Date of Death	
Place of Death	
Cause of Death	
Widow's Name	
Widow's Place of Birth	
Date and Place of Marriage	
Children	

Other Claimants to Pension & Relationship to Deceased	
Residence after Service Street/City/State	
If Veterans Hospital/Home, Name/Street/City/State	

Source _____

Microfilm No. _____ Roll No. _____

Microfiche No. _____ Card No. _____

If not from original document, fill in below.

Source (if not book) _____

Book Title _____

Author _____

Publisher _____

Publication Date _____

Volume & Page No. _____

Passenger Arrival Form

Name of Passenger	
Date of Birth	
Place of Birth	
Name of Ship or other mode of transport	
Date of Departure	
Port of Origin	
Date of Arrival	
Port of Entry	
Last Residence	
Citizenship	
Occupation	
Destination	

FAMILY MEMBERS

Sex	Name	Age	Place of Birth

Source _____

Microfilm No. _____Roll No. _____

Microfiche No. _____ Card No. _____

If not taken from original document, fill in below.

Source (if not book) _____

Book Title _____

Author _____

Publisher _____

Publication Date _____

Volume & Page No. _____

Naturalization Record Form

Name	
Date of Birth	
Place of Birth	
Last Address Outside U.S.	
Alien Registration No.	
Name of Ship	
Port of Departure	
Date of Departure	
Port of Entry	
Other Mode of Travel Used to Enter U.S.	
Date of Arrival	
Name Used at Time of Entry	
Name Used on Naturalization Cert.	
Naturalization Certificate No.	
Name of Naturalization Court	
Location of Court	
Residence at Time of Naturalization	
Street	
City & State	

Source _____
Microfilm No. _____ Roll No. _____
Microfiche No. _____ Card No. _____

If not taken from original document, fill in below.

Source (if not book) _____
Book Title _____
Author _____
Publisher _____
Publication Date _____
Volume & Page No. _____

F12

1790 Federal Census

State _____ County _____ City/Town _____

Post Office _____ Page _____ Microfilm/Microfiche No. _____ Roll/Card No. _____

Book Title _____ Line(s) _____ Author/Editor _____

Publisher _____ Publication Date _____ Volume No. _____ Page No. _____

Heads of Families	Free White Males Over 16	Free White Males Under 16	Free White Females	All Other	Slaves	Miscellaneous

1800/1810 Federal Census

State _____ County _____ City/Town _____ Post Office _____

Page _____ Line(s) _____ Enumeration Date _____ Microfilm/Microfiche No. _____ Roll/Card No. _____

Book Title _____ Author/Editor _____

Publisher _____ Publication Date _____ Volume No. _____ Page No. _____

Heads of Families	Free White Males					Free White Females					All Other Persons Except Indians	Slaves	Miscellaneous
	Under 10	10-16	16-26	26-45	45 up	Under 10	10-16	16-26	26-45	45 up			

1820 Federal Census

State _____ County _____ City/Town _____ Post Office _____

Page _____ Line(s) _____ Enumeration Date _____ Microfilm/Microfiche No. _____ Roll/Card No. _____

Book Title _____ Author/Editor _____ Volume No. _____ Page No. _____

Publisher _____ Publication Date _____

Names of Heads of Families	Residence	Free White Males						Free White Females					Foreigners NOT Naturalized	No. occupied in			Male Slaves				Female Slaves				Free Colored Males				Free Colored Females				Miscellaneous
		Under 10	10-16	16-18	18-26	26-45	Over 45	Under 10	10-16	16-26	26-45	Over 45		Agriculture	Commerce	Manufacture	Under 14	14-26	26-45	Over 45	Under 14	14-26	26-45	Over 45	Under 14	14-26	26-45	Over 45	Under 14	14-26	26-45	Over 45	

1830/1840 Federal Census

State _____ County _____ City/Town _____ Post Office _____

Page _____ Line(s) _____ Enumeration Date _____ Microfilm/Microfiche No. _____ Roll/Card No. _____

Book Title _____ Author/Editor _____

Publisher _____ Publication Date _____ Volume No. _____ Page No. _____

Names of Heads of Families	Free White Males													Free White Females													Miscellaneous
	Under 5	5-10	10-15	15-20	20-30	30-40	40-50	50-60	60-70	70-80	80-90	90-100	Under 5	5-10	10-15	15-20	20-30	30-40	40-50	50-60	60-70	70-80	80-90	90-100	

1850 Federal Census

F16

State _____ County _____ City/Town _____ Post Office _____

District/Ward/Beat _____ Post Office _____ Page _____ Line(s) _____

Enumeration Date _____ Microfilm/Microfiche No. _____ Roll/Card No. _____

Book Title _____ Author/Editor _____

Publisher _____ Publication Date _____ Volume No. _____ Page No. _____

Dwelling No.	Family No.	Names of Residents	Age	Sex	Color	Occupation	Value of Real Estate	Birthplace	Married in year	Attended school	Can't read/write	Impairment	Miscellaneous

1860 Federal Census

State _____ County _____ City/Town _____ Post Office _____

District/Ward/Beat _____ Post Office _____ Page _____ Line(s) _____

Enumeration Date _____ Microfilm/Microfiche No. _____ Roll/Card No. _____

Book Title _____ Author/Editor _____ Volume No. _____ Page No. _____

Publisher _____ Publication Date _____

Dwelling No.	Family No.	Names of Residents	Age	Sex	Color	Occupation	Value of Real Estate	Value of Personal Estate	Birthplace	Married in year	Attended school	Can't read/write	Impairment	Miscellaneous

1870 Federal Census

F18

State _____ County _____ City/Town _____ Post Office _____
District/Ward/Beat _____ Post Office _____ Page _____ Line(s) _____
Enumeration Date _____ Microfilm/Microfiche No. _____ Roll/Card No. _____
Book Title _____ Author/Editor _____
Publisher _____ Publication Date _____ Volume No. _____ Page No. _____

Dwelling No.	Family No.	Names of Residents	Age	Sex	Color	Occupation	Value of Real Estate	Value of Personal Estate	Birthplace	Father's birth-place if not U.S.	Mother's birth-place if not U.S.	Month born in year	Month married in year	Attended school	Cannot read	Cannot write	Impairment	Eligible to vote

1880 Federal Census

State _____ County _____ City/Town _____

District/Ward/Beat _____ Post Office _____ Page _____ Line(s) _____

Sup. Dist. No. _____ Enumeration Dist. No. _____ Enumeration Date _____ Microfilm/Microfiche No. _____ Roll/Card No. _____

Book Title _____ Author/Editor _____ Volume No. _____ Page No. _____

Publisher _____ Publication Date _____

House No. & Street	Family No.	Names of Residents	Color	Sex	Age prior to June 1	Month of birth if born census year	Relationship to head of household	Single	Married	Widowed	Divorced	Married in census year	Occupation	Cannot read	Cannot write	Birthplace	Father's birthplace	Mother's birthplace

1900 Federal Census

F20

State _____

District/Ward/Beat _____

Sup. Dist. No. _____ Enumeration Dist. No. _____

Book Title _____

Publisher _____

County _____ City/Town _____

Post Office _____ Page _____ Line(s) _____

Enumeration Date _____ Microfilm/Microfiche No. _____ Roll/Card No. _____

Author/Editor _____

Publication Date _____ Volume No. _____ Page No. _____

House No. & Street	Family No.	Names of Residents	Relationship to head of household	Race/Color	Sex	Month born	Year born	Marital Status	Years married	Mother of how many children	Of these, how many living	Birthplace	Father's birthplace	Mother's birthplace	Year of immigration	Years in U.S.	Naturalization	Occupation	Mos. unemployed	Mos. att. school	Can read	Can write	Can speak English	Own or rent	Own free or mort.

1910 Federal Census

State _____ County _____ City/Town _____

District/Ward/Beat _____ Post Office _____ Page _____ Line(s) _____

Sup. Dist. No. _____ Enumeration Dist. No. _____ Enumeration Date _____ Microfilm/Microfiche No. _____ Roll/Card No. _____

Book Title _____ Author/Editor _____

Publisher _____ Publication Date _____ Volume No. _____ Page No. _____

House No. & Street	Dwelling No.	Family No.	Names of Residents	Sex	Race/Color	Age	Marital Status	Years Married	Mother of how many children	Of these, how many living	Birthplace	Father's birthplace	Mother's birthplace	Year of immigration	Years in U.S.	Naturalization	Can speak English	Occupation	Can read	Can write	Attended school	Own or rent	Own free or mort.	Farm or house	Union or Confederate Civil War Survivor	Impairment